Cornerstones of Freedom

The Story of
VALLEY FORGE

By R. Conrad Stein

Illustrated by Ralph Canaday

CHILDRENS PRESS™

CHICAGO

Library of Congress Cataloging in Publication Data

Stein, R. Conrad.
   The story of Valley Forge.

   (Cornerstones of freedom)
   Summary: Describes the encampment of the Revolutionary
Army at Valley Forge and recounts how the soldiers sur-
vived a winter of hardship to continue the war against
the British.
   1.   United States—History—Revolution, 1775-1783—
Campaigns—Juvenile literature.   2.   Washington, George,
1732-1799—Headquarters—Pennsylvania—Valley Forge—
Juvenile literature.   3.   Valley Forge (Pa.)—History—
Juvenile literature.   4.   Valley Forge National Historical
Park (Pa.)—Juvenile literature.   [1.   United States—
History—Revolution, 1775-1783—Campaigns.   2.   Valley
Forge (Pa.)]   I.   Canaday, Ralph, ill.   II.   Title.
III.   Series.
E234.S83   1985   973.3'341   84-23203
ISBN 0-516-04681-0

For General George Washington and the American army, 1777 was the most frustrating year of the Revolutionary War. Earlier, Washington and his troops had been driven out of New York and begun a long, dismal retreat across the plains of New Jersey. The relentless British advance was so discouraging that it moved patriot Thomas Paine to write, "These are the times that try men's souls."

Late in the year, the British marched on Philadelphia. At the time, Philadelphia served as the capital of the infant American republic. General Washington believed that the fall of the city would be a disaster for the nation. Determined to stop the British, he moved his army to a Pennsylvania stream called the Brandywine.

On September 11, 1777, a deafening roar rocked the banks of the little river as both sides exchanged cannon fire. When the smoke of the explosions cleared, waves of British soldiers swept out of the woods and splashed across the river. The red-coated troops pointed their muskets forward, and their long bayonets glistened in the sun. The river valley was swept with the ugly sounds of battle. Terrified horses neighed. Wounded and dying men screamed. The booming voices of commanders thundered out orders. Cannon blasts sounded like the devil's own drumbeats.

From atop his horse, General Washington watched and worried. He knew that the British outnumbered his men, but from what he could determine, the Redcoats seemed to be advancing with only small units. Was the main force behind those small units? Did the British commander consider Washington's army to be so trifling a foe that he was attacking with only half his soldiers? Through noon the awful battle raged on. The once clear water of the Brandywine flowed red. And General Washington worried.

Suddenly, a deadly hail of musket fire burst out of the trees behind the American lines. Redcoats by the

thousands swarmed down on Washington's men. The Americans were trapped between the river waters and the charging British.

In an instant, George Washington realized his mistake. The British commander, General Howe, had preoccupied the Americans by sending small bands of soldiers across the river. Meanwhile, the main body of Redcoats curved upstream and crossed

the Brandywine at an unwatched point. General Washington cursed. The British had used the same tactic a year earlier when driving the American forces out of Long Island, New York. Worse yet, Washington had stationed scouts along the upper banks of the Brandywine, but no reliable word of a British crossing came forth. In war, ignorance of the enemy's movements is usually fatal.

The battle at Brandywine almost became a rout. Only Washington's skilled generalship prevented a disaster. He sent his best division to engage the British forces that stormed the American rear. Then he led an orderly withdrawal of the main body of American troops. By nightfall, the Americans had at least escaped annihilation.

Still, Brandywine was another depressing loss for the American army. It also served as a bitter taste of the horrors of war. An American private named Elisha Stevens summed up the day-long ordeal in these words: "The battle at Brandywine began in the morning and held till night without much cessation of arms, cannon roaring, muskets cracking, drums beating, bombs flying all around; men [were] a dying, wounded [men's] horrid groans [were enough] to grieve the hardest of hearts. . . ."

The defeat left Philadelphia open to the British army. On September 26, 1777, the Redcoats marched into the American capital. It was a staggering blow for the new nation. All over the country people spoke in hushed tones, whispering to each other that American soldiers would never be a match for the British professionals.

During the early stages of the Revolutionary War, the American army suffered from two dismaying shortcomings. First, its officers had no experience fighting European troops. Previously, the Americans had fought against Indians. The Indian wars called for entirely different tactics than doing battle with well-drilled, well-armed Europeans. Second, the American soldiers were amateurs compared to the British Redcoats. The Americans lacked the ability to maneuver and march in precise formation as could the British.

But the American army, despite the string of defeats it had suffered, retained remarkable spirit. Even the lowliest private had a profound belief in the rightness of his cause. While the beaten soldiers fell back from the Brandywine River, a captain named Enoch Anderson wrote, "I saw not a despairing look, nor did I hear a despairing word. We had solacing words always ready for each other — 'Come, boys, we shall do better another time.' Had a man suggested, or even hinted the idea of giving up, he would have been knocked down. . . ."

Soon the winds turned icy and sleet rained down on the Pennsylvania pine trees. With winter approaching, the British troops made themselves comfortable in the warm homes of Philadelphia residents. General Washington, on the other hand, faced the momentous decision of choosing winter quarters for his army of eleven thousand men. Washington could move his soldiers to Reading or Lancaster. But he wanted his army camp nearer Philadelphia to discourage any further British advances. So he decided to winter his troops on a desolate plain that commanded the high ground some twenty-two miles outside the city. The plain would forever be enshrined in American history. It was called Valley Forge.

The march to Valley Forge was a nightmare for the exhausted soldiers. After many months in the field, they lacked clothing, proper food, and even boots for their feet. The journey began in late December while powdery snow whistled through the ranks of the Americans. Wounded men clung to their comrades' shoulders as the long column inched

over the roadway. Valley Forge lay only thirteen miles away, but it took Washington's weary troops a full week to hike there. Many of the soldiers, whose boots had worn out long ago, wrapped their feet in rags. A bitter George Washington wrote, "you might have tracked the army...to Valley Forge by the blood of their feet."

The Americans limped onto the windswept plain called Valley Forge the week before Christmas, 1777. They saw only snow-covered pine forests, frozen streams, and empty meadows where the winds howled. It was the most forbidding place to spend a winter that any of them could imagine. A Connecticut soldier named James Sullivan Martin wrote, "We arrived at Valley Forge in the evening. It was dark, there was no water to be found, and I was perishing with thirst. I searched for water till I was weary....I felt at that instant as if I would have taken [food] or drink from the best friend I had on earth by force. I am not writing fiction, all are sober realities."

On the evening of December 23, General Washington sat in a drafty tent, surrounded by shivering officers, and wrote a long, pleading letter to the leaders of the American Congress. "What is to become of the Army this winter?" he asked. "We have...no less than 2,898 men now in camp [who] are barefoot and otherwise naked." The general then complained about Congressmen who dwell "in a comfortable room by a good fireside" while the common soldier "occupies a cold, bleak hill and sleeps under frost and snow without clothes or blankets."

Washington's letter cut to the heart of the supply problems plaguing the American army. In order to win battles, the men needed ammunition, horses, clothing, proper food, and medical supplies. But the infant American republic lacked the organization to deliver these items on a regular basis. Government officials argued as to whether the various states or

the national government should finance the war. Also, many American businessmen, who claimed to be patriots, reaped enormous profits by selling goods to the army at outrageous prices. About these businessmen Washington wrote: "I would to God that one of the most atrocious [of the profiteers] of each state was hung upon a gallows five times as high as the one prepared by Haman. No punishment in my opinion is too great for the man who can build his greatness upon his country's ruin."

Largely due to a chaotic government and unchecked profiteering, the troops shivered and starved at Valley Forge. Many officers feared that the men, despite their marvelous spirit, would finally just give up and walk home. Washington warned Congress that unless he was given proper supplies, his army "must inevitably be reduced to one of these three things: starve, dissolve, or disperse."

Still, there was work to do in the winter camp. Washington ordered the troops to fell trees and dig foundations to create an encampment of log cabins. Thomas Paine, who visited the camp as the building

got underway, described the scene: It was "like a
family of beavers, everyone busy; some carrying
logs, others mud, and the rest fastening them
together." Street by street and cabin by cabin, a
surprisingly neat little city rose on the snow-swept
fields. Not until all the men were secure in their
cabins did George Washington abandon his own
dreadfully leaky tent and move into a stone house
owned by a local farmer.

During the building of the cabins, the men
suffered from near starvation rations. While they
worked they often chanted, "No bread, no meat. No

bread, no meat!" One soldier complained that his "holiday meal" consisted of nothing more than rice and a few teaspoons of vinegar.

None of the troops had proper clothing. Their coats, trousers, and boots had worn to shreds during the summer campaigns. One soldier on guard duty was seen standing on his hat to keep his bare feet out of the snow. A regimental doctor named Albigence Wald gave this description of a typical enlisted man suffering through the winter at Valley Forge: "There comes a soldier; his bare feet are seen through his worn-out shoes, his legs nearly naked from the tattered remains of an only pair of stockings, his breeches not sufficient to cover his nakedness, his shirt hanging in strings. . . .He comes and cries with an air of wretchedness and despair, 'I am sick, my feet lame, my legs are sore, my body covered with this tormenting itch.' "

Dreadful diseases such as typhus, smallpox, and pneumonia swept the camp. The men, weakened by hunger and the constant cold, sickened and died. Before the winter ended, nearly three thousand of Washington's soldiers died of disease and malnutrition and were buried in unmarked graves at Valley Forge.

In the midst of January 1778, when Washington's army was at its lowest ebb, American General James Mitchell Varnum wrote this despairing letter: "The situation of the camp [at Valley Forge] is such that in all human probability the army must soon dissolve. Many of the troops are destitute....The horses are dying for want of forage. The country in the vicinity of the camp is exhausted. What consequences have we rationally to expect? Our desertions are...great. The love of freedom, which once animated the breasts of those born in the country, is controlled by hunger, the keenest of necessities."

Facing these outrageous conditions, many other armies would have either risen up in mutiny or deserted as a group. And, indeed, hundreds of desperate young men did flee their miserable winter quarters. Still, there was no widespread unrest among the troops. Also, for every one deserter, a hundred more stayed to fight again in the spring. Writing from a snowbound log cabin, Colonel John Brooks of Massachusetts claimed: "In my opinion nothing but virtue has kept our army together through this [winter]. There has been the great principle, the love of our country, which first called us to the field, and that only, to influence us."

A trickle of supplies began rolling into the camp with the appointment of a new quartermaster general. In early 1778, Congress asked Nathanael Greene to tackle the rugged job of supplying the American army. Greene was a loyal officer who wanted to remain with the men of his division, but he accepted the job of quartermaster because he recognized its importance. General Greene was no miracle worker. He could not produce supplies where none existed. Yet he was tireless in rummaging through government storehouses and sending every blanket, coat, and pair of boots he could find to the freezing men at Valley Forge. About the winter camp, Greene later told Washington, "God grant we may never be brought to such a wretched condition again."

Spring finally came to Valley Forge. To the suffering men, the gradually warmer days seemed a miracle. An even more astonishing miracle occurred in the Schuylkill River, which wound through the camp. With the breakup of the ice, the river suddenly became alive with shad. Spring warmth brought whole schools of the fish swarming through the stream. It seemed to the hungry Americans that the shad were a gift from God. Armed with baskets,

pitchforks, and even tree branches, Washington's soldiers plunged into the chilly waters to scoop out the wriggling fish. Laughing like schoolchildren, the men cleaned the fish, salted them, and stored them in barrels. Because of the huge run of shad, the army ate fish for weeks.

The camp was further cheered by the arrival of the dynamic Martha Washington. Lady Washington, as the general's wife was called, journeyed to Valley Forge in the early spring. She was a strong woman with a warm smile. Her visits to the camp's bleak hospital did more to comfort the sick than had the doctors' many medicines.

The greatest boost to the morale of Washington's men came from Europe. Since the war's beginning, European intellectuals and idealists had looked upon the American Revolution as a great crusade. In the American wilderness, a backward, colonial people were attempting to establish a bold new society. The society intended to reject the Old World practice of

Casimir Pulaski

Marquis de Lafayette

Thaddeus Kosciuszko

Baron Von Steuben

kings, queens, and powerful landlords ruling over the masses.

Most of the European idealists who came to America were themselves Old World aristocrats. Nevertheless, they entertained the radical belief that a person should be judged by his character instead of by the family into which he had been born. Many were experienced army officers who hoped to teach Americans how to fight against European professional soldiers. From Poland came Pulaski and Kosciuszko. From France came the young Marquis de Lafayette, who grew to idolize George Washington. And from Prussia came an old warhorse of a soldier, the Baron Friedrich von Steuben.

Baron von Steuben had served as an officer under the brilliant Prussian leader Frederick the Great. Although his military career had ended long before he came to America, von Steuben was skilled at teaching precision marching to infantrymen. The ability to drill was essential when fighting the British, whose ranks of men marched into battle as smartly as if they were on a parade field. When the Baron reported to Valley Forge, Washington took an instant liking to him. Von Steuben gasped, however, when he first observed the marching ability of Washington's soldiers. They looked more like a herd of cows than an army.

Starting with a small group, von Steuben taught the men basics—the proper way to stand at attention, left face, right face, forward march, flank march. The job was exasperating. One witness wrote that the former Prussian officer grew so angry at the many mistakes made by amateur American soldiers that he began to "swear in German, then in French, and then in both languages together." Finally, he pleaded for someone to "swear for me in English."

Still, the Baron drilled the men on the muddy fields from sunup to sundown. When he was satisfied

that his first small group knew how to march, he sent them back to their units to teach their comrades. The Baron then began teaching another group himself.

Baron von Steuben was a strict drill master, but he was constantly fascinated by the unique American troops he was instructing. He quickly learned that he had to treat the free-spirited Americans differently from the quick-to-obey Prussians. In Prussia "you say to your soldier, 'Do this,' and he does it," wrote von Steuben. "But [here] I am obliged to say, 'This is the reason why you ought to do that,' and then he does it."

A new army emerged from Valley Forge in the summer of 1778. It bore little resemblance to the wretched band of troops that had limped into the camp six months earlier. Thanks to the quartermaster, Nathanael Greene, the army was better equipped. Thanks to the influence of von Steuben and the other Europeans, both the officers and men were more professional. Moreover, everyone from private to colonel felt that their dreadful winter experience at Valley Forge had made them better soldiers. They marched out of the camp convinced that since they had endured that terrible winter, they surely could take anything the British could give them.

Finally, none of the men would ever forget that their general, George Washington, had suffered through the miserable winter at their side. After a succession of depressing defeats, many soldiers had begun to doubt the leadership ability of their commanding officer. But seeing Washington sharing their hardships at Valley Forge day after day convinced the men that they could follow this commander to the end of the war.

Washington's leadership ability shone during the Battle of Monmouth, the army's first encounter after Valley Forge. During the vicious fighting, a large American unit began to retreat. Washington met the fleeing Americans, and according to the Marquis de Lafayette, his "presence stopped the retreat...his calm courage gave him the air best calculated to excite enthusiasm." Lafayette told how Washington galloped his horse "all along the lines amid the shouts of the soldiers, cheering them by his voice and example, and restoring to our standard the fortunes of the fight. I thought then, as now, that never had I beheld so superb a man."

At the Battle of Monmouth, the British realized

they were no longer fighting against the ragtag
soldiers they had faced during the disastrous year of
1777. Suddenly and shockingly the amateur
Americans had become professionals commanded by
an outstanding leader. For Washington's men the
bitter lessons of Valley Forge had reaped a great
reward.

George Washington's Headquarters

Today, Valley Forge, Pennsylvania is a sprawling park that covers more than two thousand acres. The original stone house that served as Washington's headquarters still stands there. Rows of log cabins have been carefully reconstructed as replicas of the ones that once housed eleven thousand half-starved men. The park serves as a memorial honoring those courageous men who stood with George Washington during their country's darkest hour.

Thomas Paine

From 1778 on, the American army marched forward to victory and eventually won independence for their nation. But the period of peril that was climaxed by the painful winter at Valley Forge will always be remembered in the words of the powerful writer of the revolution, Thomas Paine: "The summer soldier and the sunshine patriot, will, in this crisis, shrink from the service of his country; but he that stands it now, deserves the love and thanks of man and woman. Tyranny, like hell, is not easily conquered; yet we have this consolation with us, that the harder the conflict the more glorious the triumph."

About the Author

R. Conrad Stein was born and grew up in Chicago. He enlisted in the Marine Corps at the age of eighteen and served for three years. He then attended the University of Illinois where he received a bachelor's degree in history. He later studied in Mexico, earning an advanced degree from the University of Guanajuato. Mr. Stein is the author of many other books, articles, and short stories written for young people.

Mr. Stein now lives in Chicago with his wife, Deborah Kent, who is also a writer of books for young readers, and their daughter Janna.

About the Artist

Ralph Canaday has been involved in all aspects of commerical art since graduation from the Art Institute of Chicago in 1959. He is an illustrator, designer, painter, and sculptor whose work has appeared in many national publications, textbooks, and corporate promotional material. Mr. Canaday lives in Hanover Park, Illinois, with his wife Arlene, who is also in publishing.